# Best Friends Through the Years

Charlotte Ruth

Title: Best Friends Through the Years
By Charlotte Ruth
ISBN:  978-0-578-34025-8

Subjects: 1. Family & Relationships/Friendship
2. Family & Relationships/Life Stages/General

Cover Designer:  Debi Lindhorst
Photo credits: Charlotte Ruth, author, personal album, 2021

# TABLE OF CONTENT

# Best Friend

As we start out in life, we all want to have a *best friend,* and that is what this story is all about. In fact, just to be sure I have the right definition, I have gone to several dictionaries to get the right definition.

According to Urban Dictionary, *friend* means, "A friend is someone you love and who loves you, someone you respect and who respects you, someone whom you trust and who trusts you. A friend is honest and makes you want to be honest, too. A friend is loyal."[1]

Yet, that same dictionary, Urban Dictionary, says *best friend* means:

1. A best friend is someone who is there for you through thick and thin. It's someone who listens and understands you.

2. Someone you can call anytime about anything you feel you need to 'tell' or 'vent'. It's someone who will stand up for you in the times when you need it most, keep your secrets close, and someone you can trust with your life.[2]

Barton Goldsmith, Ph.D., in his article in *Psychology Today* "10 Ways to Be a Best Friend," lists ten important factors that come into play. One factor is "Being emotionally supportive. This is probably the most important element of any adult friendship. Best friends refrain from unnecessarily criticizing each other and tend to be nonjudgmental." Another factor is "A best friend will listen to you and thoughtfully respond rather than react to what you've said even if you have triggered something in him or her. The ability to hear what another is truly saying is one of the best parts of friendship." The third factor I want to mention is "Best friends go out of their way for the people they care about, and it feels good to both parties. You can tell who your real friends are when you need help with a move or a ride to the airport." The final factor I think is important is "Thoughtfulness is a quality that deepens and strengthens any friendship. Being able to see someone else's needs—and to do what you can to fulfill those needs—enables bonding experiences."[3]

As you read all of the transcriptions of what a "Best Friend" is, it comes down to how well you get alone and share each other's secrets, ideas, trust and love for each other.

Because I have spent several years working at the Boys and Girls Club, I have seen children from kindergarten age group through mid-high school, and I have heard a lot of best friend stories. In fact, it gave me the passion to tell my story of all of my best friends through my lifetime.

# Best Friend #1

My first best friend that I remember was kind of ironic because it was my mother's best friend's youngest daughter, Cindy. She lived about two blocks from me, and she was a year younger than me. We went to the same grade school but were in different grades.

I was unable to walk to school with my best friend Cindy because my parents had me walk with my five brothers and one sister to school every day. And Cindy had to walk with her brother and sister to school. Since there were no school buses for us back in the 1950's to take us to school, and maybe having us walk together to school was a security thing for the parents.

But I was able to see Cindy on weekends and spend time with her. We would have sleepovers at her house at least once a month, which was a lot of fun for several reasons.

1. Her house was bigger than mine, which gave us more room to play (There were nine of us living in a three-room house with no running water and no inside bathroom.).

2. She had more toys than I did (we didn't have the extra money to spend on a lot of toys, so this was amazing to me.).

3. It was also a lot quieter at her house than mine because she only had one brother and one sister living at her house, so it was much more enjoyable (I had five brothers and one sister.).

4. Plus, we also went to the same church, which we both enjoyed very much. And that probably brought us closer together knowing we both believe in our Lord above. And sometimes even our mothers or should I say, all four of us, would spend time together, which was always good times. Because we know how busy parents can be and not have enough time for kids these days.

The closeness continued on with my best friend for about five more years because that is when my first best friend Cindy moved out of town with her mother to another town not too far way.

I was very sad, and if you think about it, you would have been sad as well. You see, kids at school always made fun of me because of what I wore. They thought I was dirty all the time. My best friend loved me for me not for what she wanted me to be, or what they wanted me to be but for who I was. So, when your best friend moves away, and you lose contact with her, and then all of a sudden year go by before you have found new "best friends," you feel alone. Or you feel that years have gone by, but they haven't really before you really do find a new best friend but the sadness says with you.

This, however, was not the end of our best friend

relationship. My mother and I made several different trips to

their new location for visits off and on. But then I had a

shocker when my best friend got married and moved to

Chicago.

This was hard for me to believe because coming from a

real small town and moving to one of largest cities in the US.

WOW - Well to tell you the truth I was not far behind her.

When I turned twenty-two years of age; I also was feed up

with this small town I lived in but for a lot of other reasons.

So, I contacted Cindy and asked her if I could come to

Chicago and live with her and her new husband until I could

find a job. And of course, she said "YES".

It wasn't very long, maybe three weeks, and sure enough,

I did find a job, not too far from where I was living. And

Cindy and her husband decided to move to the suburbs to

be closer to his job. So, I just stayed where I was and took over their apartment. I was so happy at the time, new apartment, new location, new job, what could be better than this.

But then time goes on and yes, you do make new friends, but are they or will they be a best friend? However, you still miss your family, that is living several hundred miles away from you.

The catalog distribution company that I was working for in Chicago had some real wonderful people working there, and I was lucky enough to find a couple of nice ladies that I became close with at work and started running around with them.

About two years of living in the Big Windy City, I was ready to move back home. Missing everyone back home from the small town, I called my wonderful father, and he came to Chicago, picked me up, and moved me back home.

Once again, I lost contact with my first best friend Cindy. But years later after I had moved back home and had been married about 14 years, Cindy's mother passed away, and I went to the funeral in our town and made contact with Cindy again.

In fact, Cindy even came out to my house. We sat and talked for a while to reminiscing about old times. Unfortunately, I have not seen her since.

You can never forget your first best friend for the fact that the friendship will last for over 60 years, and you learned so much together, like love – thoughtfulness – loyalty – trust – someone who listens to you and understands you, because that is what a real best friend is all about.

# Best Friend #2

After my older brothers and sister stopped walking me to

school because they went onto higher grade levels or they

just plan quit school, and my first best friend Cindy moved

away, I really needed someone else to be my second best

friend. I found another best friend that I started walking to

school daily for a couple of years, and her name is Deb.

Deb only lived about a block away from me so was easy

to get to her house and then on to school. She lived with just

her mother, sister, and brother and was a classmate of mine.

I walked with her and her sister and brother to school daily.

Plus, in the early 1960's, we didn't have lunch at school, and

we couldn't carry a lunch bag, so we had to walk home to

have lunch and then back to school for our afternoon classes.

The sad thing is what I thought or who I thought was a

second best friend only lasted a couple of years. You see it is that age time frame when kids like to make fun of other kids,

so Deb took their side and began to make fun of me. So, you

see, again, I was that classmate the kids liked to make fun of.

My family did not have much money to buy a lot of clothes,

so my classmates would call me dirty and smellie and make

it into a song and at recess sang it to me every day.

But then again that is what kids do, even in today's day

and age. I know that now, but it sure was hard to accept at

the time when you have a classroom of kids making fun of

you, and you are all by yourself. It's hard to hold inside and

in fact hide your true feelings, that is for sure.

Bottom line, who you thought was your best friend

turned out to be not a best friend. But then again, that is how

we grow and learn what a best friend is.

Or maybe Deb just got tired of walking to school with me

and didn't know how to tell me. So, I definitely needed to

find a new "best friend." I never had any contact with her since that either.

But here are signs of a bad best friend: A bad friend has no self-control and doesn't care about the consequences of telling your secrets to others. Spilling these secrets could embarrass you or bring harm to you which are things a good friend would never intentionally do.

The sad thing is you can't tell a ten-year-old how to detect a bad best friend. They have to go through the pain themselves and live with it and try in time to forget and forgive.

# Best Friend #3

Here I am 10 years old playing in my back yard that Dad finally put up a basketball hoop, and a girl from across the alley came into my yard and asked if she could play ball with me, well of course I said "yes".

Her name is Lisa, and we quickly became third best friends. We played ball quite often, that is as long as my five brothers would let us, and if they wouldn't, we would go for a walk around the neighborhood. And sometimes go into her house and play with her dolls and toys.

The really nice thing about her family was her father worked at the drive-in theater, and they would get to see the movies free, so they would let me go with them, but they would have to sneak me in by either putting me in the trunk or hiding me under blankets on the back seat floorboard.

This was heaven for me. I never got to do anything like this before. We never had the money to go to the drive-in theater. And another thing, when the fourth of July came, that was much more fun with them because of all the fireworks they had.

The friendship was good and fun, and then it was gone, just like that after a couple of years in the neighborhood. Her parents got a divorce and moved on the other side of town, and we went to different schools. And I never saw her much after that. After she graduated from high school, she moved away, and I have not seen her since. How quick friendship goes away.

Of course, in the beginning of your friendship, you always think this one will last forever, and then forever never comes, it just goes away, and you have to start looking for another best friend and hope the next one will stay

forever.

15

# Best Friend #4

Well, I did find another classmate of mine that I could call my fourth best friend, and that only lived five or six blocks from me, and her name is Sue. So, I would walk to Sue's house in the mornings and then we would walk onto school from there.

You see, Sue and I were kind of from the same home level you might say. She lived with her mother, one sister and one mentally challenged brother. But we really enjoyed each other's company and Sue turned out to be a very good fourth best friend of mine for many years of my life and still currently is one of my best friends.

At the time we were growing up, we were strictly best friends by walking back and forth to school daily not a whole lot of weekend together time, because by the time I turned thirteen, and I started going rolling skating at least three times a week, and she just wasn't into skating.

In fact, while I was roller skating, I may have found my fourth best friend and possible another best friend which I will mention at another time. The best friend #5 at the time was my sister's sister-in-law but let me get back to my best friend #4 Sue.

We continued to go to the same school and high school and in fact, we graduated the same year. And I wanted in the worst way to get an apartment and move away from home once I graduated from high school, so I asked Sue to move into an apartment with me and she did. You know how it is, your eighteen, you know everything, you are smarter than your parents, and you just have to get out on your own.

However, four months after we moved into an apartment, she wanted to move back home because her boyfriend proposed to her, and she wanted to save money, so they could have a nice wedding.

The only thing bad about her moving back home is, I could not move back to home because my mother would not let me. She was so mad at me because I wanted to move out on my own, in the beginning. I guess because she didn't think I was mature enough she said, "if you move out now you can never come home again." Trust me that hurt. I had to find a place to live in a short period of time.

So, with the job that I had at the time, I knew I could not afford an apartment, so I had to look for a sleeping room. Lucky I was able to find one in rather quickly and stayed there for another six months until finally my mother said I could come back home.

As I said earlier, I am still good friends with this best friend #4 Sue, but now she is retired and has moved to a southern state. But we still exchange birthday cards and

Christmas cards every year and is taking life easy, and I am

happy for her.

Sue has been a good best friend throughout sixty years

and was there for me when I needed her most, but again that

is what best friends do.

# Best Friend #5

Barbie – Katye – Not really sure if I can call these two girls my best friends or not. But age twelve and in the seventh grade, they were really friendly to me, and they kept asking me to spend the nights at their homes. Wasn't sure if again they were going to make or create an incident to make fun of me in front other classmates, but I did take them up on several offers and boy did I have a great time. Of course, I couldn't offer the same overnight stays at my house, but it didn't seem to bother them.

Being a backwards and shy person in my own self not really sure, what would happen next with these two new best friends. They were smart in school and it was as if they decided to take me under their wing and be nice to me as if to make up for all the years, they were not. Again, still not sure how to take them but this really built up my self-

esteem.

Well then, the basketball games started at school, and

they were cheerleaders for the "A" team, which was good,

but they said they were looking for a "B' team cheerleader.

So, they talked me into running for a cheerleader, and I

made it. I did enjoy it that season because it was something I

had never done before, plus I felt everyone was starting to

like me and not make fun of me at school anymore.

This happened for one more year through our last grade

school year, and it was all good. But then we all moved on to

high school, and we kind of lost track of each other. But

whenever I did see them through life, they were always

good and kind to me, which I really appreciated. And even

now when I saw Barbe at a garage sale, she mentioned that

we should get together, so I gave her my business card, so

she can call me when she has time.

Life is good, and people and especially kids can change.
That made a world of difference to me and changed my

outlook a lot towards other kids too when they started to

accept me finally in school.

# Best Friend #6

As I stated earlier, I met my best friend #6 Hannah at the skating rink, and in fact, it was my sister's sister-in-law. We would walk to and from the skating rink several times a week and talk about different things and just have a good time at the rink. We never spent any time at my house because she was kind of a homebody person. And as you got to know her, you would know why.

We did go to different grade schools but did start out at the same high school; however, then she quite high school at an early age of seventeen. Which I could not understand, but that was not for me to judge.

You see Hannah came from a strange family, and this is my opinion too, her mother and father both were alcoholics. I am not sure how being raised in that environment would feel. In fact, her father was killed coming home one night drunk, he hit a set of gas tanks and everything blow up. So sad to lose your father like that at a young age and everyone knowing how he died.

After Hannah quite high school, she found a job in a factory, and we continued to go roller skating for a total of three years. But then she found a boyfriend and got married and had a couple daughters and a son. It is like she wanted to grow up really fast.

I lost contact with her after her mother passed away, and she divorced her first husband, and she moved out of town. And then at an early age of sixty, she herself passed away.

But I must say, I was proud to know her son and talk to him until his passing at an early age of thirty from cancer. The main thing about best friends is to always be there for them in time of need because you don't always know what is really going on inside that person and what their goals are in

life.

25

# Best Friend #7

My best friend #7 Marie, I didn't know in school even though we went to the same school because we were in different grade levels. Marie was the same age as I but was held back because of an illness early in her school years because of missing too much class time.

We did meet when she and I started working at our town hospital in the kitchen and soon became best friends. We worked a lot of evening hours after school and weekend hours doing dishes, cleaning off tables and delivering food trays to patients. It was a pretty easy after school job, and we meet a lot of good people there that we enjoyed working with.

Marie had a boyfriend in high school, and she spent a lot of time in and out of that relationship the whole time we worked together. But when she was out of the relationship for the twentieth time, I was there for her to help her

through it because that is what friends do. But I did happen

to say, "Marie you are going to break up one to many times,

and he won't come back," and that indeed did happen.

We left working at the hospital and went to a factory to

work after we both graduated from high school. At that

point I worked days at one factory and second shift at

another factory so I kind of loss contact with Marie for a

while.

But she didn't waste any time on finding a new boyfriend

and started dating again. And eventually she married him

and was blessed with two lovely daughters.

I since moved on or should I say moved out of this small

town and onto Chicago for a couple of years just to get out of

the relationship I was in and out of.

However, when I did move back to this small town again, I found the love of my life and married him and, in fact, we moved in a house right across the street from Marie.

Since we just lived across the street from Marie, we were able to spend a lot of time together off and on. And one day I was extremely happy that she was home because I let my five-year-old son play out in our fenced in yard, by himself while I was inside doing laundry. When I heard a knock on the door and it was Marie, and she had my son. He had opened the fenced door and crossed the street and went to her house to play with her daughters. Boy was I extremely happy that she was there for me.

Needless to say, our lives go through a lot, and Marie's just changed when she got a divorce from her first husband, but I was there for her. We would go out together and have several talks, walks and drinks, along with long drives home. Comforting and being there for her was the main objective.

Marie found a new husband and started a new life after her divorce. Talking with the daughters, they seemed to like him okay. And so, their life went on for a few more years. Marie's mother and father owned the house she lived in and her parents did live right beside her, but they were ready to move out into the country as they did.

Once Marie divorced her second husband, she also was ready to move out into the country beside her parent's house in a trailer. Which was good because shortly after she moved there, her father passed away, so she was there to care for her mother.

A few years later, we both changed jobs and started working at the same company. Marie worked out in the factory, and I worked in scheduling the production for that plant, which we both enjoyed very much.

Maybe five years into this new company we were working at, one morning while I was at my desk, someone from the production floor came up to me and told me that Marie did not come into work that day, they said that she was found at home passed away trying to call someone. I was heartbroken losing a best friend of over thirty years like that at an early age of forty-six and also just thinking of what her daughters are going through right now.

Needless to say, I was there for her daughters when they needed me. And told them if they ever needed anything, please let me know; I would be there for them.

I did keep in contact with one of the daughters on social media, which made me feel complete. The other one had moved out of town, so I had not heard from her for a long time.

Just the other day Marie's sister passed away, and I did go the funeral home, and there they were Marie's daughters. We hugged and hugged some more then talked about old times for over an hour.

I know this is ironic, but six months later, Marie's other sister passed away. Once again, I went to the funeral home to console Marie's two daughters and Marie's mother who I wonder how is holding up through all of this loss.

We again exchanged contact information, so we could keep in touch. That is what friends do.

# Best Friend #8

Let me introduce to my best friend #8, her name is Ruth. We worked together at our small-town Hospital in the kitchen doing dishes.

Ruth was the cashier at the food line for the kitchen at the hospital while I did the dishes from the patients from upstairs. We would walk to and from work together several times a month.

We talked a lot, and I would tell her about my other friends I have, but what was always sad to me, Ruth seemed to put them down a lot. This just didn't seem right to me; in fact, each time we would walk together to work, I almost didn't know what to talk about, so I just let her do all the talking.

Ruth did talk about her family a lot. She had a very slim sister with a very good personality, and a younger brother that just was mischievous, but no father figure in the picture.

So, I just kind of when with letting her do all the talking for a

while.

Finally, I had had enough and just came right out and

asked Ruth, what she had against my other friends because

whenever I would talk about them, she would always put

them down. Well, her remarks were, in fact she didn't like

them and if I wanted to be best friends with her, I had to lose

all of my other friends. Because I was only able to have one

best friend and that would be her or no friendship with her

at all.

This is more like a bad best friend, someone who is

trying to take over your life and control who you could or

could not be friends with. This is not what friendship is all

about. No one should ever tell you who you can make

friends with. Because this feeling goes back at least for me because I never had a lot of friends growing up and I really

wanted them now more than ever.

So, I ended this best friend right away but continued to

be friendly with her to this day forth.

# Best Friend #9

Kyle was probably only about eleven years old when I started letting him be my skating partner at our south end of town roller rink. We skated together really well, and we both enjoyed it very much. His mother and father owned the skating rink, and I tried to go there at least three times a week because it gave me such enjoyment.

This skating rink was a very popular place to go for kids of all ages and wasn't very expensive either. At least my parents were able to pay for me to go, and the owners were wonderful people, or should I say good people persons.

We are talking back in the 1960's time-frame when we really didn't have much to do, and this skating rink was the perfect place to go. The owners seemed to keep all the riff raft under control, and like I said, Kyle the son of the owners would become my ninth best friend.

Most of the other kids in town went to the YMCA where they had 50's/60's music in their basement every Saturday night, and the kids did a lot of dancing, but these kids were not from my side of town, more like the ones that use to make fun of me. So, I was more for the roller-skating type of fun, same type of music and good times.

There would be weekends when Kyle and his family would go out of town to a different skating rink adventure, and they would take me with them. Here again, I was in heaven, I enjoyed every minute of their time they spent with me.

I was thinking that maybe Kyle after a while had a crush on me because here, I was sixteen and he was eleven, but then the bigger boys stated noticing me, and Kyle didn't really like that. So, he started backing away.

But the bigger boys were the kind of boys that were, how do I want to say mischievous? And getting into small town trouble, either with alcohol or theft. So, they too would come and go. And once again, I was back with my skating partner Kyle.

But then time goes on and I was turning twenty-one and had a boyfriend for about three years now, off and on, more off than on. And working two jobs so not really having much time to go skating. I then decided to move out of town to Chicago for a couple of years and lost all contact with Kyle and most of my friends.

However, I returned to my small town, two years later, and heard that Kyle found a real girlfriend and married her, and there was a baby on the way. I was really excited for him and his new family to be.

Shortly after returning home from Chicago, I was living with my youngest brother, and that year another one of my brothers set me up on a blind date, where I met my husband, and when I introduced him to Kyle the following year, he also was happy for me.

It had to be at least ten years later when Kyle's mother was on her death bed at hospice. Kyle contacted me and a few other close friends to let us know that his mother wanted to say her goodbyes to a lot of the skating rink kids. When I went up there, there must have been a line at least a block long to see her.

Everyone that knew her wanted to be able to say their goodbyes to her because she was such a wonderful person. This lasted a couple of days, and I was there two days with Kyle to help him through this. What this town lost that day.

Kyle and I are still in contact with each other at least two if not three times a year because he comes back home here from the southern state he lives in to visit his sister and brother, and I also believe his daughter, and of course, to see me.

Keeping in good contact with each other is what friends do to always show you still care about each other.

# Best Friend #10

My best friend #10 is Joan that again I worked with at the small-town hospital in the kitchen doing dishes and eventually with me becoming the morning breakfast cook.

By the time Joan started at the hospital kitchen, I final was out of school and had a car, and because she lived in a smaller hometown about fifteen miles away, we were always on the road after work and on weekends.

We mostly hung out in Joan's small town because her father was the sheriff there. Which meant we had to be good right? NO not us. Joan was the first person that taught me how to taste alcohol. Of course, we could not get caught and or tell anyone who or where we got the amazing drink either that would be so wrong.

These were good times traveling back and forth with Joan. She was a lot of fun and had a very good personality not just as friends but also a very good person to work with. That is very important too. That is where you sometimes meet your best friends at work.

This friendship continued for a while, but I only stayed at the hospital through the age of nineteen, and then I moved on to an office job and lost contact with Joan but left in good standing with her.

If fact, I saw her just the other day at my house, and we hugged as if it were yesterday. Missing all those years as friends, but now we are friends on the internet. And yes, she has not changed at all; same wonderful person she ever was.

# Best Friend #11

Well, here I am young and naïve, living in an apartment that needs two incomes. So, I met who I thought was my best friend #11, Kitty.

We didn't work together because Kitty worked in the restaurant business, and I worked in an office for a very large company in this small town. But we had a lot of fun together and going to movies and driving around town, which was a big thing for everyone to do back in the late 1960's.

Kitty didn't really have a steady boyfriend and then again neither did I. What I am trying to say is my boyfriend was as you say "on again off again" relationship. But at the time Kitty and I we're living together, my boyfriend and I we were on again.

However, one afternoon when I got off work, I came home as usual. Walked up the stairs, opened the door and there was Kitty and my "on again" boyfriend hugging and kissing so tightly that they did not hear me come in the door.

Well, needless to say, things did not go well at all. Words were flying and so were my arms and hands. Kitty moved out and so that was the last time I saw that boyfriend.

Once again, signs of a bad best friend: A bad friend has no self-control and doesn't care about the consequences. And I think that is all I can say about this friendship.

# Best Friend #12

Ellie turned out to be a very good best friend of mine, and to tell you the truth, I can't remember how we met. She was five years younger than me and went to a Catholic school even her five older brothers I never knew either. But that doesn't matter, the fact is we did indeed become best friends even to this current day.

Ellie was not even a skating person, mainly we just drove all around town from one end of town to the other, looking and flirting with guys. Because back in the 60's that is what you did in these small towns.

Once I got my apartment, Ellie would come and spend weekends with me, and one thing that turned out to be really ironic was she started dating a kid or should I say guy that I use to babysit for. WOW!

As I have said several times, I moved to Chicago around the age of twenty-two, and during my stay, Ellie came to live with for a couple of weeks because she needed to have an abortion. It was not for me to judge her but to be there for her, and the state she lived in did not have abortions available for women.

When she went back home and turned eighteen, she got married to the same guy I use to babysit for and the father of the baby she just aborted. When I moved back home from Chicago and got married myself, we both had our first child only two months apart and then our second child two days apart. What are the chances on that?

But then a couple of years later, Ellie and her family decided to move out west. Ellie had three brothers that already lived out west, and she and her family wanted to move out there to start a new life.

We did keep in contact with each other frequently, then her mother was diagnosed with Alzheimer's, and that was a long and hard road for their entire family. Even more when she passed away.

Ellie was still living out west when my boys were twelve and nine, and we decided to fly out west to see her and her family. Boy was that a lot of fun for the kids and myself, just being able to see my best friend again. We only stayed a couple of days, but it was something that the kids will never forget. The beauty of it all and the reconnection of their friendship with her children as well.

It took Ellie about five more years before she got a divorce and decided to move back home. However, only one of her children would be coming back with her, and that was her daughter. Her son wanted to stay with his father out west. Ellie was ok with that and moved back home.

She was able to get a job right away when she came back in town, and can you believe it, also found a boyfriend at the company she was working for. Soon after that they got married, and things started working out well for her. And I was very happy for her; she had met a great guy.

Ellie's daughter soon graduated from high school, the same year as my youngest son. We had parties, and then my son moved on to college in the southern state, and her daughter moved back out west for a while with her father, which made Ellie depressed for a while, but then she got better.

Ellie's daughter only stayed out west with her father a couple of years, and then she moved back with her mother. But took her time to find a job but still continued to live with Ellie and her husband.

Sad to say that Ellie lost her husband shortly after her husband lost the retail company, they were both working at. So, a couple of things hit her hard at the same time. She soon became depressed again and locked herself in her room for days. I went over and tried to comfort her as well as her daughter, but nothing seemed to work. Finally, we had to just make her go to the doctor and get some medication for what she was going through.

She finally came through or kind of back to normal. Then because of no income coming in, she had to sell the house and try and find an apartment she could afford to live in.

Again, her daughter was not working, or if she was, it was only for a few weeks off and on a job, moving to different jobs all the time. Then Ellie was able to be approved for disability and that helped out a lot.

This on again off again in the job market with her daughter was not going very well at all, but then her daughter found a boyfriend to marry her, and they had a couple of kids.

Now Ellie was doing good on her own. I would go over and take her out to lunch on the weekends and talk for a couple of hours, reminiscing about old times. As life goes on, that's what we do to bring back the good times only.

About ten years have passed and now Ellie's daughter has been divorced and wanting to move back in with her mother. So, she let her, of course. But Ellie is not the same; she is starting to forget things, like names, contacts, phone numbers and so on, kind of like her mother did when she was diagnosed with Alzheimer's. Her daughter did, in fact, take her to the doctor, and for sure that was what they diagnosed Ellie with.

I went over to see her and asked her what was going on, and her daughter told me. I looked at Ellie and asked her if she knew me, and she said yes. I said do you know my phone number and she said yes. I told her to start calling me more often so we can get together. Well that never happened; in fact, her daughter took away her phone so she couldn't call, plus moved out of the apartment they were living in and never told me where they moved to. I looked high and low for them.

I have lost all contact with my best friend #12. I have even contacted one of her brothers to try and find out where she was, and he did not know either. How cruel is that? This daughter must not have any friends at all and for sure no "Best Friends."

Will this daughter let me know when she passes? I guess I will have to wait and see.

# Best Friend #13

Chicago best friend 1972 -Jamie

As I said earlier, shortly after moving to Chicago and living with my first best friend, I found a job at a catalog distribution center just a few blocks away from where I was living.

Thinking about it moving to this tenth largest city in the US, was I really going to find what I would call a "best friend"? Well, we will see, inside this small company I started to work for, there were some really nice people to work with, and some that would come forth and show a little bit of friendship right away. And the way it turned out was there was two really nice ladies that wanted to be my friends and take me out to lunch the first week that I was there so, I accepted.

After my best friend #1 and her husband that I was living with left the city and moved to one of the suburbs and left me here alone, I did feel the need to become a little bit closer to my two co-workers Jamie and Diane.

After a few months of the three of us chatting back and forth and going out to lunch together and learning about each other a little bit, I kind of weeded out one of them and became best friends with Jamie and her husband Ed.

We would go out to lunch, as a lot of co-workers do, and we would go out one or twice a week at a local bar in the evenings to spend some social time together. And then we started also spending time on the weekends too, sharing our time together. They would even try to set me up on dates, but what I had been through in my hometown with my old boyfriend, I was not ready for any dates, that is for sure so I turned them down.

Every once in a while, a couple of old friends that I knew from my skating rink times would look me up in the "Windy City" to say hi, and I was really excited about that also, seeing them as if I was back home.

I do remember very clearly just driving down a highway with my windows down and the air blowing in my 70 Opal GT, and a police officer pulled me over. I couldn't understand why he was pulling me over because I know I wasn't speeding. He did not ask for my driver's licenses, all he said to me was, "Mam roll your windows up, you are in a bad part of town." All I could say was "thank you" and do what the officer said and went on my way home there in Chicago. But this stuck with me for a while, trust me, coming from a very small town, as the song goes "everybody knows your name."

I would go home maybe once a month or every six weeks just to see mom and Dad along with family especially around the holidays because when you are by yourself, you do and need to be with family.

One day I was at my desk working, and I looked up and out the window, and all of a sudden, I screamed. What happened! My car was pushed up under another car. So, a big Semi came around the corner at a rate of speed and hit it and pushed it under another car. Sadly, to say I did not have insurance, so I lost my transportation to and from work and back and for to my family back home. Whenever I did go back home, I would have to take a bus, and that was a lot longer and more expensive too.

But after about two years have gone by living in Chicago, I had decided to move back home, so I called my best friend Clair to see if I could move in with her, and she said "yes."

So, I said goodbye to my best friend Jamie and told her that I would see her in later years. As I did.

About two to three years later, my husband and I met her in Chicago which he had never been there before coming from a very small town. And it was so good for me to see Jamie again, but I would only see her maybe one more time, as we did in another two years later, we met Jamie with her new husband at a casino new Chicago.

Which again was good to see her not knowing that would be my last time of contact with her. But good friends are there for sure when you need them, and that is what counts.

# Best Friend #14

I was working two jobs at an early age of nineteen or twenty, days in a factory on a production line, in a really small town about seven miles away and then nights in my town testing army radios. This second shift job I met my fourteenth best friend Clair.

We would go out in our cars on supper brake and have our snack, or at least I would, Clair was a little bit more creative than I was. She had a line of alcohol set up in her car that all she had to do was pull out the line and pour into a glass and drink it for supper brake. I told her that was too cool.

We got to be best friends right away, and her husband didn't even mind. We would go to the beach or reservoir and lay out all day. Or even on the weekends go bar hopping, and I wasn't even twenty-one yet, but nobody knew that of course.

But it wasn't all about the bar hopping or the drinking, it was the time spent together, and the time we spent with her children, we both enjoyed together.

Well then, my second shift job was laying off, and they offered me a chance to work in the office on days, and of course I said "yes." More money and I was able to quit my first shift job in the factory and only have to work one job that paid almost as much as both of them. The only bad thing was I would not be around Clair daily. She would have to find another job somewhere else because they closed down second shift.

We were still able to spend time together, and we continued on for at least two years back and forth with the kids spending time with them, going to the reservoir and most of all bar hopping with me. Until Clair became pregnant, and her husband was not sure it was his, well I would not say.

Clair was there for me, and I would always be there for her no matter what. But then it was time for me to move on to Chicago as I have said many times. Missing my best friend very much.

But after about two years have gone by living in Chicago, I had decided to move back home, so I called my best friend Clair to see if I could move in with her, and she said "yes of course."

But since I moved in with Clair and was seeing my old boyfriend again plus working a second shift job, things were a little bit different. In fact, it made a little different kind of stress on our friendship. Clair didn't like my timing of late hours on with my job, and then my boyfriend would come

in the house late, so she asked me to move out, and trust me
that hurt more than you will ever know. I thought best
friends would do any and everything for you. OH Well.

So, I moved in with my brother and his girlfriend. After
that point, I never saw my current boyfriend again. I guess it
was that on again off again time. Well, I didn't come back to
live that kind of life again, that is for sure, so I indeed gave
that boyfriend up for sure.

Three months went by, so, at that time, my other brother
asked me if I wanted to go on a blind date? I said yes. But
my girlfriend Marie worked at the same grocery store that
this "blind date" person did. So, I went to Marie and asked
her to point out who this person was, so I would and could
get a look at my blind date for that following weekend, and
she did. And four months later I married him.

For about six to eight years went by before I made friends again with Clair. I guess because it hurt me that she would put me out like that. And I didn't know until the other day what the real reason was. It was her soon-to-be ex-husband thought she was seeing my ex-boyfriend. And if the traffic flow of cars didn't stop going in and out of the house, he was going to take her kids away from her, or he was going to get violent with her. Knowing that now, well I would have moved in a minute for her, never wanting to put her in that kind of situation.

Things got a lot better between us, and she was bartending in a city nearby, and I would go and visit her about twice a month when she was working.

What a pair of either best friends or good old drunks, that should not have even been on the road. When we would go out together, if I was driving and my car would go off the road, she would move the steering wheel back on the road, but if she was driving and she would go off the road, I would push the wheel back on the road. That's what friends do. Please nobody ever try this.

I just thank God we gave all of that silly drinking issues up and started concentrating on raising our families. However, she is the lucky one with all her children and grandchildren right in the same town with her, where mine are either in the same southern part of this state or south western part of the US that we only see once a year.

But Clair and I have been friends for over fifty years, and we see each other at least once a month, to keep in touch. I drive by her house about four times a week and under my breath tell her I love her, and how grateful I am that she is my best friend.

# Best Friend #15

As I stated earlier one of my brothers asked me if I wanted to go out on a "blind date?" I said yes. But after he told me where this guy worked, I knew that my best friend Clair also worked there, so I went to ask her to show me what he looked like just to see if I really wanted to go on this "blind date." And after seeing what he looked like, I did indeed decide to go ahead and go with my brother and his wife on this date and meet Darth.

This was a holiday weekend in the fall of the year, and we dated all weekend, and we connected right from the start. In fact, he asked me over to his trailer where he lived to see if I would cook him a dinner, and I said I would. But once the dinner was done, I pulled it out of the oven, carefully I thought, but it fell onto the floor. Wow was that embarrassing. But we picked it up and cleaned it off along with laughing about what just happened and still had a good dinner.

We dated every weekend for about a month before Darth took me home to meet his parents and his kids. You see, he had two boys from a previous marriage. And those boys were absolutely adorable.

Of course, I still had to get my father's approval of him to continue dating. But that wasn't until Thanksgiving dinner that Dad gave his approval that I could continue seeing Darth, you see I was what they say "daddy's little girl."

Needless to say, Darth and I got married in December of that same year; in fact, we went to the same location that my other two brothers got married at that same year in the southern states.

Our first born came in early summer that next year, and in fact, he was about three weeks early, but he was beautiful, and we were proud to introduce him to the other boys.

I guess you could say we were really in LOVE and best friends, and that we tried hard to be a good family of five. This continued for a few more years until our second son was born, and we were again proud to introduce him into our family.

For about three more years, we would still have just visitation on weekends with our sons from Darth's first marriage, but then they decided to move to a southern state, and sadly to say, we had no say about them moving at all, so they picked up and left right away.

Sure, we missed the boys because they moved down south, terribly, but here at home we still took our early vacations to Disney Land and beach side travels with our boys we had at our home. Life must go on.

We would pay to have the boys fly home to see us in the summertime for about three more years. And we would also go places with all four boys in nearby states that we know would be fun, like one Great America park also a variety of other amusement parks and lakes.

Then the oldest son from Darth's first marriage decided that it was time to spend time with his father, so he moved in with us from his southern state. We were in heaven. Enjoying his company, knowing him all over again especially in his teenage years.

Then it was the last six months before the oldest son was going to graduate from high school and his brother decided to come up from the southern state and move in with us also. This just could not be true, please pinch me. But he did and we had all four boys together again. That was the most wonderful feeling any parent could have.

But all good things must come to an end as they say, and it did. After graduation, both boys decided to move back to the southern state again with their mother.

What can you do? They are big boys now, old enough to make their own decisions. We said our goodbyes and didn't get to see them until that next summer when we drove to their location.

But as they say, "life goes on," but you still miss your children, no matter how old you are or they are.

Darth and I decided to go on a cruise. It was on a three day one because our younger boys were with a sitter, Darth's sisters. So, we had to hurry back home.

If there ever was a "Best Friend," that would be my husband. At this stage in life, we had already been through a lot. We had already lost both of our fathers, and now our older boys were here for a while and now have moved back with their mother.

Like I said, the older boys are back in the southern state and decided not to go onto college but to get a job. And then get married. Then the babies started coming. Our first grandson was from our oldest son. And our next son got married, which we all attended and at the southern state. Then to our surprise, our first granddaughter came along then.

Things back home are still going strong except for Darth and my oldest son. He has a wonderful personality but doesn't want to do anything in school. He goes everyday but puts no effort in his studies, so the principal asked for him to quit. Does that make since?

He was able to get a job and move out on his own, which was good because that is what he needed to show maturity. Then he met a wonderful lady and moved in with her for a while. Now they were going to have a baby, our first grandson. How exciting was that?

Our youngest son went on to college and graduated with grade point averages. But found the love of his life there at college, and he decided to get married and live in the southern part of the state we live in.

Well, we are/were experiencing empty nest syndrome, and my best friend Darth and I needed once again to get away and go on another cruise. Which we did, but this time it was a five-day cruise. Altogether, we have been on five cruises, and I want to go on at least two more.

Well, the kids are doing great and getting married and having grandkids for us which we are enjoying very much.

Darth and I are really close to our fiftieth wedding

anniversary. I have had a very blessed life with him, my love

and my best friend. He is my heart and soul.
69

# Best Friend #16

When I came back Chicago, I went to work in a factory again but got word that they were looking for someone to work in their Production Control department at the plant I use to work at a few years ago, so I checked it out and they hired me.

It wasn't until after I had my oldest son that we moved to the same street that Kay lived on, not knowing her. But when I went back to work at that plant, that is when I met Kay, she had started working there while I was off having my son, and she worked for the Quality Control managers. I liked her right away and to find out we lived across the street from each other was great.

At the time, Kay had two daughters and one son just going into their teens and no husband but needed a friend. So, I tried to be there for her.

It wasn't but maybe a year later that Kay did find another great man, I guess you could say he is her best friend. Because they have been married let's just say over forty years right now and are still as much in love today as they were back then, just like Darth and me.

Kay unfortunately got laid off, and she had to find another job, and we moved to a different part of town after my second son was born. So, Kay and I lost a few years of contact.

We would always, however, remember each other's birthdays and would go out for breakfast or lunch just to spend some time together and reminisce about old time and new times to come.

# Best Friend #17

Once again meeting Annie as a coworker at a company that I worked at for years. We became best friends right away and would run around together and even go and have a few drinks with my best friend Clair where she worked.

We would go to bingo a few times a month, and then her husband at the time did an amazing job of a hand portrait of my husband and my two son's that even though they are adults now, I still display this portrait on my wall to this day.

Annie got a divorce and her husband moved to an upper state in the US, and she has never seen him again. She never had any children by him, but she was very upset with the outcome of the marriage. That is when Annie and I spent more time together so friends could comfort her and be there for her when she needed comfort.

Annie and I left the same company and went our separate way; I went to an electronics company and she went to, I believe, an automotive company. Oh, we are both in the same town and we still send each other birthday cards.

How do I know she is my best friend because I know in my heart that if I needed her, all I have to do is pick up the phone and give her a call, and she would be right there for me. That is how I know.

# Best Friend #18

Moving from this big Production Control Department to an automotive company scheduling two production plants and supervising two customer service people I was able to meet Nelly. Our friendship took off right away. We would go to bingo together and go shopping together as well as many other things.

When they closed that facility, I moved on to an electronics company here in town again in scheduling and production. And Nelly went on to selling housing, which she currently does now and enjoys very much.

Nelly also does a lot of work for animals as well, and she works with me and my crafts to donate items for auctions to raise money for animal shelters.

Nelly and I were close as friends; in fact, she really touches my heart when she would buy me things for my birthday that said just that like a jewelry music box that says, "Friend Life is more fun with you in it" Or a picture frame that reads "Friend two are better than one for if they fall one will lift the other."

And another that reads "to my friend – Of all the people in my life, from beginning to end. You've been a special blessing, my dear and faithful friend, you've filled my life with laughter, Shared sorrows, joys, and tears. You've stood by me and held my hand. Walked with me through the years. When I needed someone to listen, I knew you would always be there when I weathered the storms of life you were always the one who cared. So, in this circle we call life from beginning to the end I was blessed to have you beside me my dear and faithful friend. How special is that. That is what friendship is all about."[4]

We currently go out to bingo at least twice a year on our

birthdays to celebrate and spend time together. Her life, of

course, is busier than mine because of her children and

grandchildren living in town or at least close by. But bottom

line, we do make time for each other when we needed to be

with each other, and we always will.

# Best Friend #19

Finding my best friend #19 was quite easy; Betty worked at a café that Darth and myself frequent weekly. She was a very good bartender with a good personality. That is if she liked you.

Betty new me and my family as I was growing up, so we had somethings in common to talk about good and bad, but that always breaks the ice when you see them for the first time in a long time. So, from that time going forward, we became best friends.

Betty was the type of person that if she didn't like you, she wouldn't talk to you, or if you made her mad, she sure would let you know it. Which I admired her for that.

We also had another thing in common that we could talk about and share feelings about, and that is the loss of a child. She had lost a son and Darth and I had lost our first-born son. And that is something that no parent should ever have to go through.

Betty and Darth and I would go to different taverns on the weekends and just have a good time and enjoy each other's company.

One day Darth and I decided to go to Las Vegas to do some serious gambling, so we asked Betty and another friend Ben to go with us. Boy did we have a great time. Something you will never forget, that is for sure.

Then Betty had a man friend herself which you might even say he was her "best friend." Which was a very good thing to watch because this best friend of hers changed her a lot. And you always want your friends to be happy.

That continued on for about ten years, and then Betty got word from his daughter that her best friend had passed away so we were there to comfort her and stand by her for a long time to help her get through this.

Betty continued to bartend at our favorite hangout until she turned eighty, and then one early afternoon, her daughter called me and told me that Betty had passed away in her sleep. Bless her heart! Lord if there is the most comforting way to go that is.

Trust me when I say she is to this day dearly missed by all.

## Best Friend #20

After getting laid off from my purchasing job at a large electronics company, I went to a small publishing company as a telemarketer. Not really crazy about this job, but I stuck with it. But I was able to meet Candy and became best friends with her.

For almost three years, we would go to lunch together every day and just have fun and talk about different things. Her son was autistic, and they had special games that he played in, and Candy invited me all the time to come to watch, as I did. You see, I have a grandson who is special as well and very dear to my heart.

I did take this one more step further and asked Candy if I could help raise money for these events by getting someone to sponsor a craft show, and she said yes. We were able to keep the same sponsor for four years and raised a lot of money for the Special Olympics.

After our sponsor passed away, it was hard to find someone else to take over the sponsorship, so we have not done another craft show since, but we will continue trying at a later date.

Candy and I still keep in touch and go out to lunch together every now and then. And, of course, we are friends on social media.

# Best Friend #21

Some people might say, "Why are you calling your brother your 'Best Friend'?" Well, I can tell you several reasons:

1. He is my brother for over seventy years.

2. He is a little slow, not really autistic but he has always needed a little help along with way.

3. He is the person that introduced me to my husband of forty-seven years. So, I have a lot to be thankful for.

4. Now that he is incarcerated, he really needs and depends on me know, and that is what friends do. They're there for you when they are needed.

When we were young and growing up, he is the one person that protected me from my other four brothers. And as we grew, he watched out for me from all the other neighborhood kids.

He was always a hard worker, but if he had a dime, he

would try and spend a dollar. That was just how his whole

life was, so he always turned to me, and I was always there

for him as I always will be forever and ever.

# Closure

A real best friend doesn't care when or if you're broke, when you're being moody, what you weigh, or the color of your hair. A real best friend doesn't care if your house is a mess, what kind of vehicle you drive, about your past, if your family is filled with crazy people, or how old you are. They love you for who you are, not for what they want you to be.

You truly can, as a rule, find them over night or at work. These friends can last a lifetime. And if you find them, you are the lucky one for now and forever.

Please, if your once best friend is still around and you can get back in contact with them, don't let any time go by. Enjoy your time together.

# Endnotes

[1] "Friend," Urban Dictionary, accessed March 2, 2021,
http://www.urbandictionary.com/define.php?term=friend

[2] "Best Friend." Urban Dictionary. Accessed March 2, 2021.
http://www.urbandictionary.com/define.php?term=Best+Friend.

[3] Goldsmith, Barton. "10 Ways to Be a Best Friend." Psychology
Today. Sussex Publishers, December 3, 2012.
https://www.psychologytoday.com/us/blog/emotional-
fitness/201212/10-ways-be-best-friend.

[4] Chambers Coxsey, Allison. To My Friend. Accessed March 20,
2021. http://mrmom.amaonline.com/poems/tomyfriend.htm.